written by QUINA ARAGON

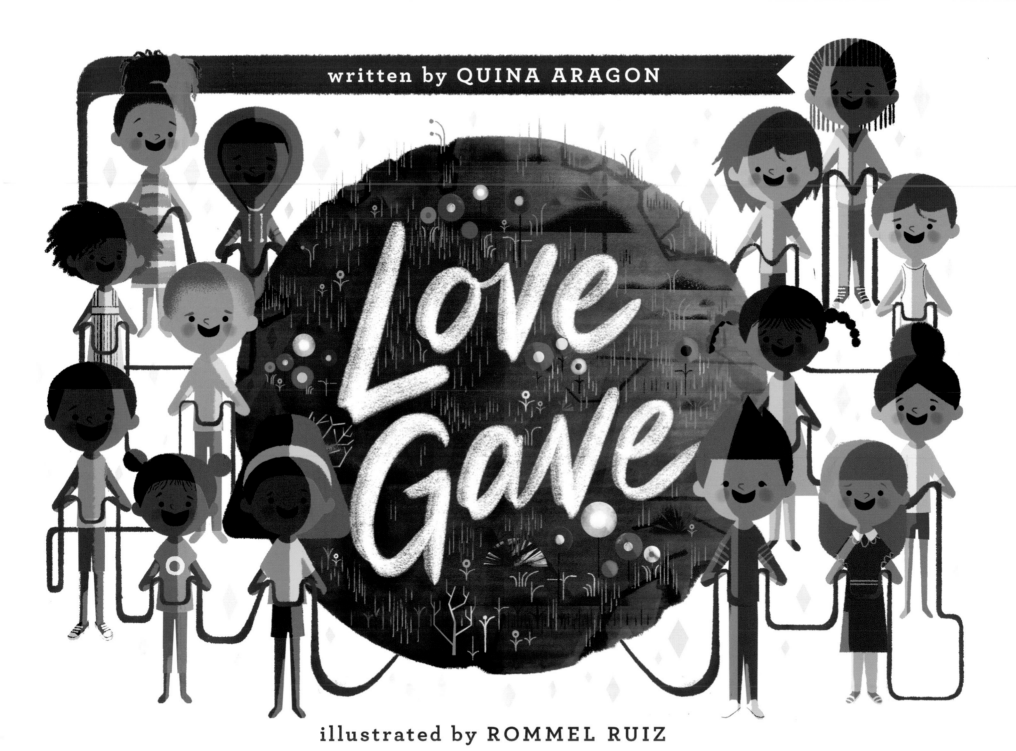

Love Gave

illustrated by ROMMEL RUIZ

HARVEST HOUSE PUBLISHERS
EUGENE, OREGON

To my sweet niece Jaelynn.
May the love of Jesus continue to bloom in your heart.

Scripture quotations are taken from the Holy Bible, New International Version®, NIV®.
Copyright © 1973, 1978, 1984, 2011 by Biblica, Inc.® Used by permission.
All rights reserved worldwide.

Cover design by Connie Gabbert Design + Illustration
Interior design by Left Coast Design
Published in association with the William K. Jensen Literary Agency

HARVEST KIDS is a trademark of The Hawkins Children's LLC. Harvest House Publishers, Inc.,
is the exclusive licensee of the trademark HARVEST KIDS.

Love Gave
Text copyright © 2021 by Quina Aragon
Illustrations copyright © 2021 by Rommel Ruiz
Published by Harvest House Publishers
Eugene, Oregon 97408
www.harvesthousepublishers.com

ISBN 978-0-7369-7438-7 (hardcover)

Printed in China
20 21 22 23 24 25 26 27 / IM / 10 9 8 7 6 5 4 3 2

Before God made
the heavens and the earth,
He lived in perfect joy.

He delighted in Himself—
One forever-existing, perfect being;
Father, Son, and Spirit
—all One.

So before time was,
there was Love.

Now,
He made us to be His friends,
but we have a big, BIG problem.
Do you know what it is?

Our greatest grandparents,
Adam and Eve,
walked away from God
in the garden of Eden.

we lie, we steal, we cheat,
and it all breaks His heart.

You see, God is perfectly clean,
like a brand-new shirt.
Our sin makes us filthy,
like we rolled in the dirt.

So the big, BIG problem is this:
God is SO good and sin is SO bad,
God and sin just can't be friends.

What should God do with us?
We have sin!

And because of our sin we should get
forever death,
forever far away from Him,
forever never God's friend,
all because of sin.

But God is love—
Father, Spirit, Son—
and Love loved so much,
Love gave us...Jesus.

Now, Jesus is God's Son,
but He was a lot like you and like me.
He loved to play, talk, and sing.

And you know what else He loved?

Children!
They'd come
for tickles and stories and hugs.

Sometimes they'd come
with messy hair and stinky feet,
but do you think
Jesus loved them any less?

Do you think
He'd first make them
take a bath?

Ha! Of course not!
He brought them close
every time

and showed them what God is like—
strong and gentle, honest and kind.

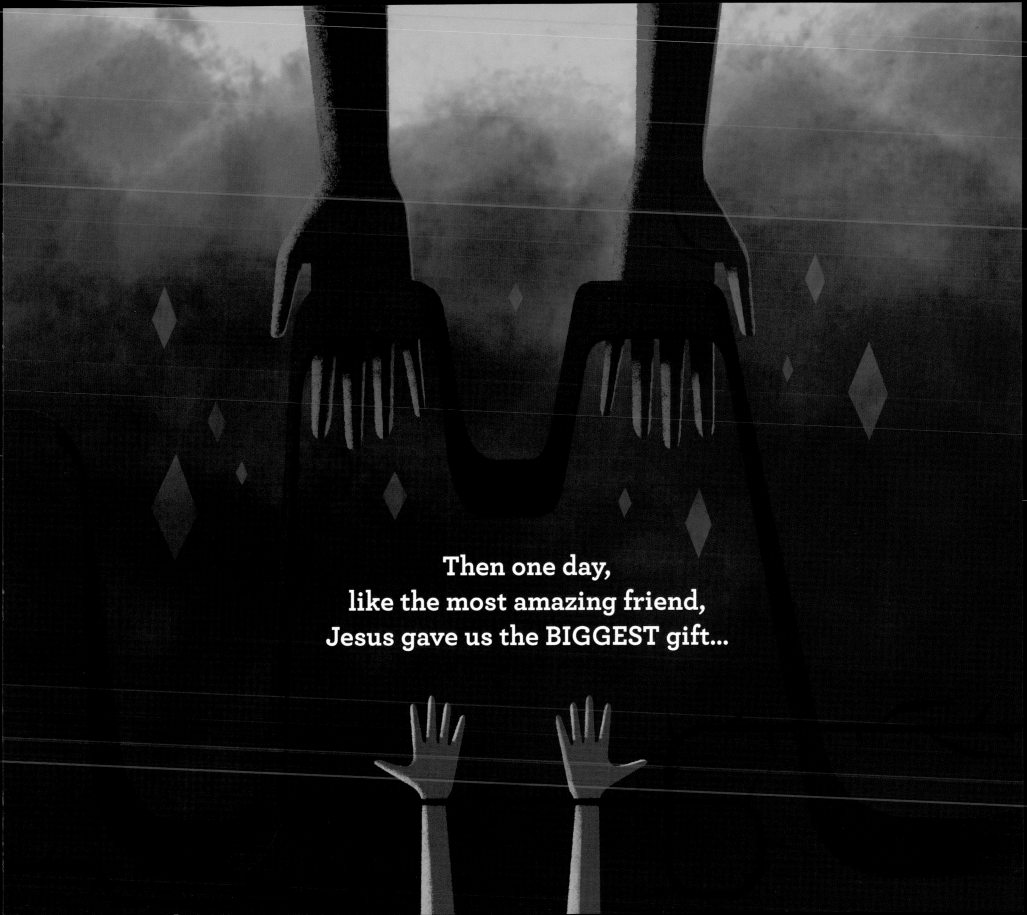

Then one day,
like the most amazing friend,
Jesus gave us the BIGGEST gift...

a gift more exciting than your wildest dreams,
a gift sweeter than all the ice cream you could ever eat,
a gift even better than a hundred presents,
a gift that cost the price of heaven.

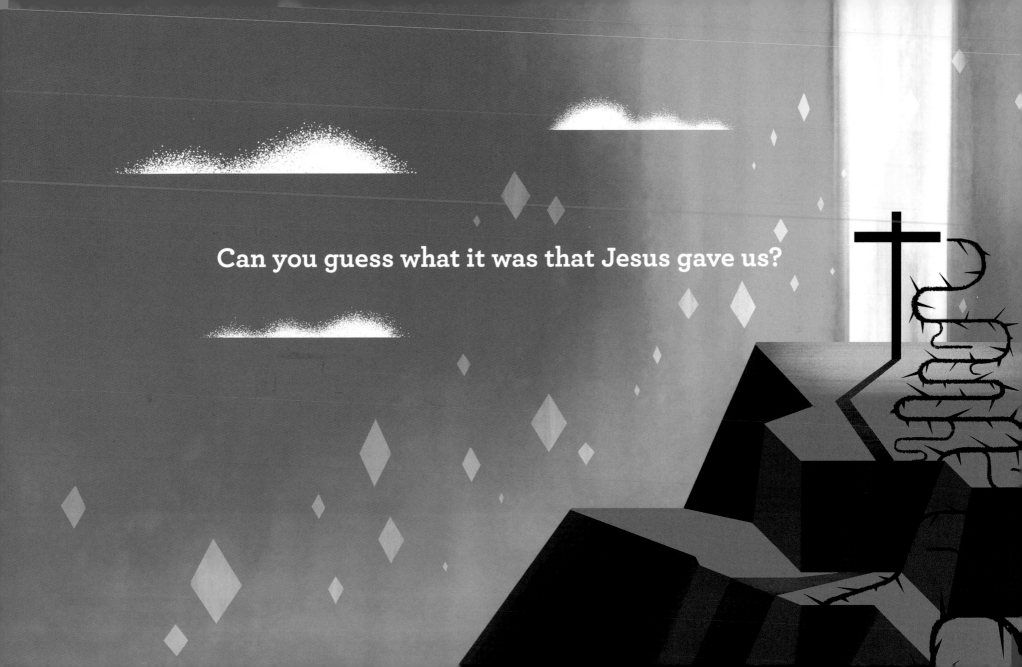

Can you guess what it was that Jesus gave us?

Jesus died and rose again
to take away all our sins
and make us His
forever friends.

You see, this gift God gave
was the greatest gift of all.
He gave us Himself.
That is love.

By trying really, really hard to be perfect?
By saving all our pennies to pay for it?
By learning a bunch of big, BIG words
like *communicable attribute*?

Be kind
to my
sister

obey
my
parents

be honest

don't say
mean things

No, no, no. None of those things will do.

Communicable
attribute

Don't you see?
God is love,

and Love is received
by anyone who will just...

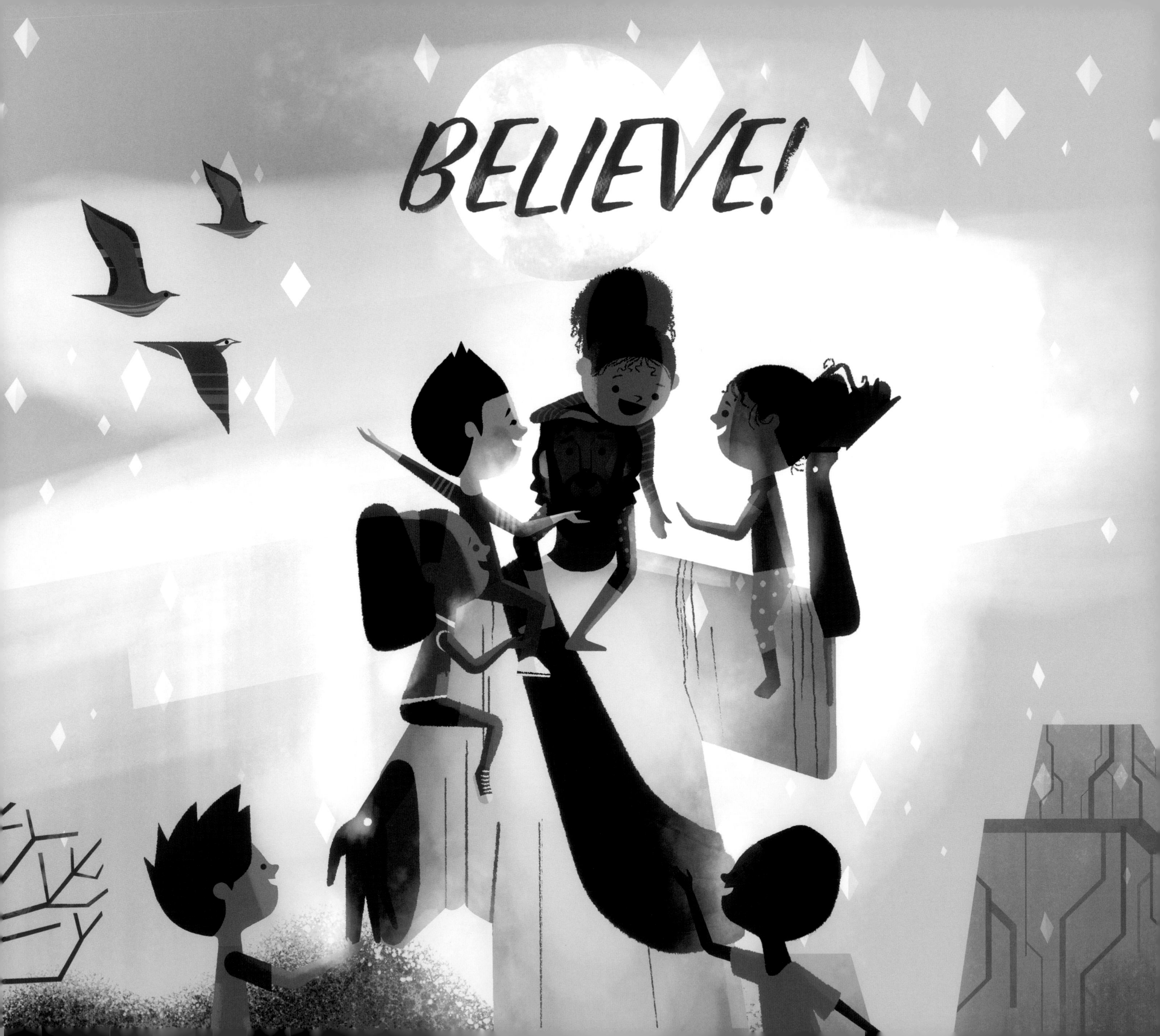
BELIEVE!

Who Can Be Friends with Jesus?

When Jesus lived here on Earth, He met lots of different people. Some had a bunch of money and toys. Others had very few toys. Some knew tons of stuff about God. Others knew very little about God. Some had lots of friends. Others had no friends at all.

But Jesus knew that our biggest problem isn't how much or how little we have. Our big, BIG problem is our sin. It keeps us from being friends with God. But it was always God's plan to show us His great love by giving us Jesus, who died for our sins and rose again so we could become His friends (John 15:13).

John, a very good friend of Jesus, told us, "To all who did receive [Jesus], who believed in his name, he gave the right to become children of God" (John 1:12). Jesus wants to be your friend too. Will you trust Him today?

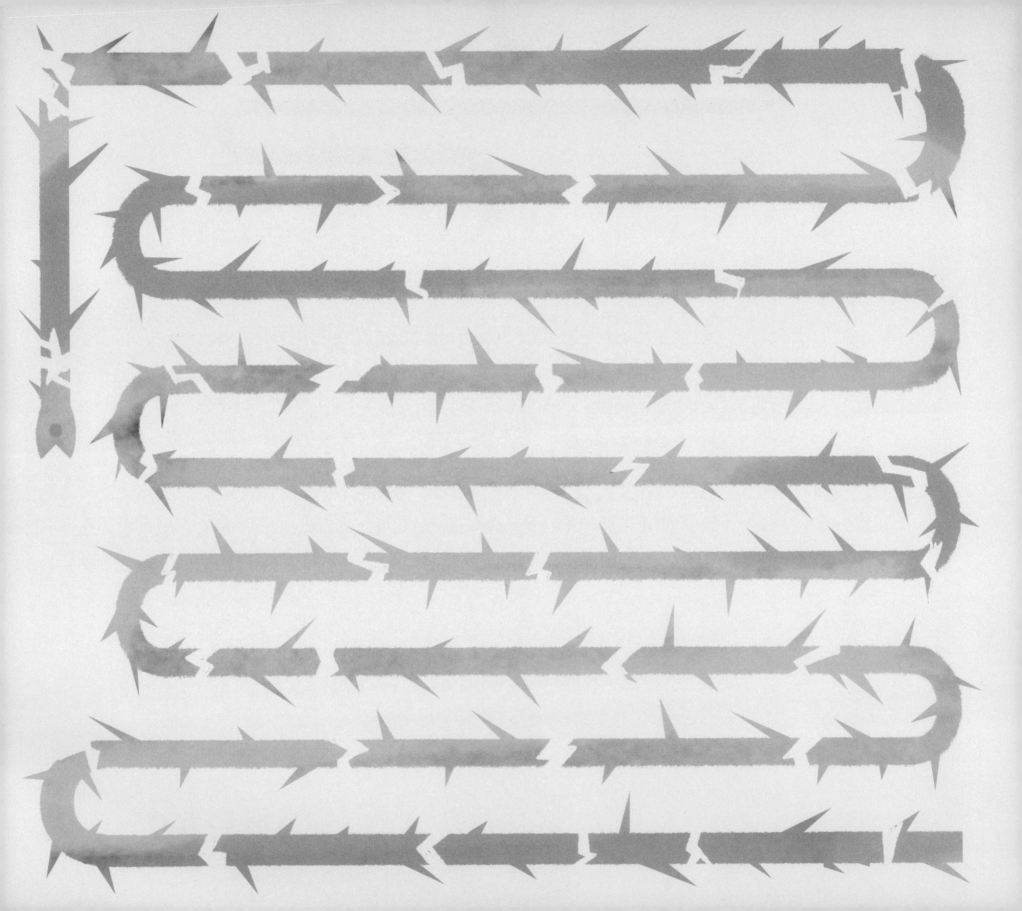